Visual Merchandising

Visual Merchandising
Best Designs from Leading Designers

From
**The National Retail Merchants Association's
Visual Merchandising Board of Directors**

PBC International, Inc. ■ NEW YORK

Distributors to the trade in the United States:

PBC International, Inc.
One School Street
Glen Cove, NY 11542

Distributors to the trade in Canada:
General Publishing Co. Ltd.
30 Lesmill Road
Don Mills, Ontario M3B 2T6, Canada

*Contact PBC International, Inc. for information
on the distributors throughout the rest of the world.*

Library of Congress Cataloging-in-Publication Data
Main entry under title:

Visual merchandising.

   Includes indexes.
   1, Display of merchandise--Pictorial works.
I.   National Retail Merchants Association.
Visual Merchandising Board of Directors.
HF5845.V54   1986   659.1'57   85-29885
ISBN 0-86636-014-X

Color separation, printing, and binding by
Toppan Printing Co. (H.K.) Ltd. Hong Kong

Typesetting by Vera-Reyes, Inc.

PRINTED IN HONG KONG

10 9 8 7 6 5 4 3 2 1

Publisher: Herb Taylor
Project Director: Cora Sibal Taylor
Editor: Carol Denby
Editorial
Assistant: Carolyn Edwins
Art Director: Richard Liu
Art Associates: Marilyn Allensbach
                    Dan Larkin

CONTENTS

M CAPWELL • ROBERT BENZIO/SAKS FIFTH AVENUE • ESSELL

RHOADS • FRANK CALISE/BONWIT TELLER • JOSEPH F DUTY

MPANY • ROBERT J. MAHONEY/ GUMP'S • ANDREW J. POU

McCLELLAND/JORDON MARSH, FLORIDA V. NA LLI

GELA PATTERSON/ BERGDORF GOODM N P

TEVE RIX/MAAS BROTHERS • HOMER SHAR HAI

RVICE SUPPORT OFFICE • KEN SPIKES/CAIN

M CAPWELL • ROBERT BENZIO/SAKS FIFTH

RHOADS • FRANK CALISE/BONWIT TELLER • PH

MPANY • ROBERT J. MAHONEY/ GUMP' A W

ENT STORES • RICK MCCLELLAND/JORDON MARSH, FLORIDA • TOM V. NATA

NELSON/Z C M I • ANGELA PATTERSON/ BERGDORF GOODMAN • ALAN PETE

RS/BAMBERGER'S • STEVE RIX/MAAS BROTHERS • HOMER SHARP/MARSHALL

NG/NAVAL RETAIL SERVICE SUPPORT OFFICE • KEN SPIKES/CAIN-SLOAN • AN

OM AZZARELLO/EMPORIUM CAPWELL • ROBERT BENZIO/SAKS FIFTH AVENUE

RAMLAGE/ MILLER AND RHOADS • FRANK CALISE/BONWIT TELLER • JOSEPH

R. JEWELL/JC PENNEY COMPANY • ROBERT J. MAHONEY/ GUMP'S • ANDREW

ARTMENT STORES • RICK MCCLELLAND/JORDON MARSH, FLORIDA • TOM V.

RON NELSON/Z C M I • ANGELA PATTERSON/ BERGDORF GOODMAN • ALAN

FOREWORD

This first edition of ''Visual Merchandising'' is designed to acquaint all levels of retail management with the fundamentals of retail visual presentation.

We have been most fortunate in being able to gather together superior examples from industry leaders as represented on the NRMA's Visual Merchandising Board of Directors.

Enjoy this publication. Study the creativity shown and allow these pages to enhance your store's visual statement. Most importantly, never forget that visual merchandising is a vital part of your store's marketing effort. It is mandatory that you coordinate your visual program with all other promotional programs within the store.

James R. Williams, President
National Retail Merchants Association

INTRODUCTION

It is safe to say that the Visual Merchandising Director's role today is far different, and certainly more important, than just five or ten short years ago. Today, the Visual Merchandiser's function is recognized as a major part of the store's overall marketing strategy.

In understanding visual merchandising, and appreciating its value to the store, management may wish to think of visual merchandising as a medium. For, as advertising presents the store externally, visual merchandising advertises the store internally.

With color, depth and mood, visual merchandising is just as much a sales medium as television, radio or the daily newspaper. Yet, unlike the traditional media, visual merchandising advertises the store (and only your commercial) 24 hours each day, 7 days every week. Hence, you might want to think of visual merchandising as the medium that does not go away after just 30 or 60 seconds.

Take a new look at your store's visual presentation and study the examples presented on the following pages. You should come away with a greater understanding of the purpose and power of visual merchandising and the contribution it makes in the overall success of the store.

John A. Murphy, Vice-President
National Retail Merchants Association

THOMAS AZZARELLO

Emporium-Capwell, *San Francisco, California*

Tom Azzarello is Vice President, Visual Presentation at Emporium-Capwell in San Francisco, California.

Azzarello started his career in retailing at Abraham & Strauss in New York. He then spent three years at Gertz, where he became manager. Azzarello relocated to Clearwater, Florida, where he was promoted to Assistant Director at Maas Brothers.

Five years later he went to Capwells as Director of Visual Merchandising. Shortly afterward, the store merged with Emporium. After two years as Director of Visual Merchandising at Emporium-Capwell, he was promoted to his present position.

According to Azzarello, "Our customer and merchandise are the primary concerns for everything we do at Emporium-Capwell." Display themes are generally contemporary — perhaps using PVC pipe or neon — reflecting the style and mood of the merchandise.

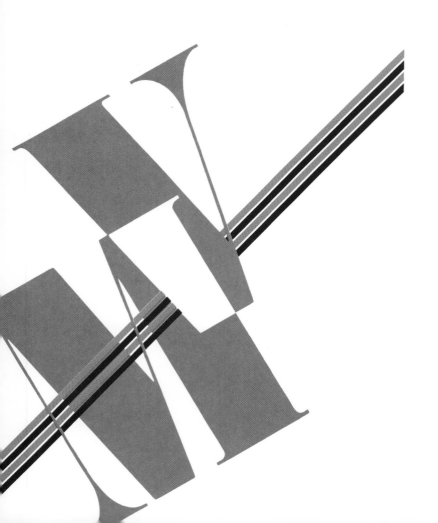

Azzarello's display work at Emporium-Capwell often features simple, graphic settings. His inventive props help the merchandise attract attention.

The theme of "Compact Living" is humorously displayed by trapping one of the furnishings available in the brightly lit cubes. The geometric shapes in the other cubes suggest a contemporary dominance.

A beautifully dressed bed is strategically placed at the entryway to the Better Linens department. Spot lights focus on each sub-section of coordinates.

A huge wall of towels created a vibrant rainbow of color. The simulated white tile wall panels were created by routing white laminate. The shower heads were attached to casually display a draped towel.

Laura Ashley bedding coordinates are beautifully displayed in the center of the shopping areas. The polished wood floor, throw rug and curtains create a cosy atmosphere.

A display window for luggage sets the mood with
the setting of an airline runway. The spectacular
colors of the sky help attract attention.

Coordinating dark wood panels, wall displayers, tables and column enclosures were created in-house for the Calvin Klein Men's Shop. Together with the brown-tinted mannequins they create a display with masculine appeal.

The entry to "The Market" is a glass-enclosed, homey kitchen display of the type of merchandise available in this housewares and gourmet food department.

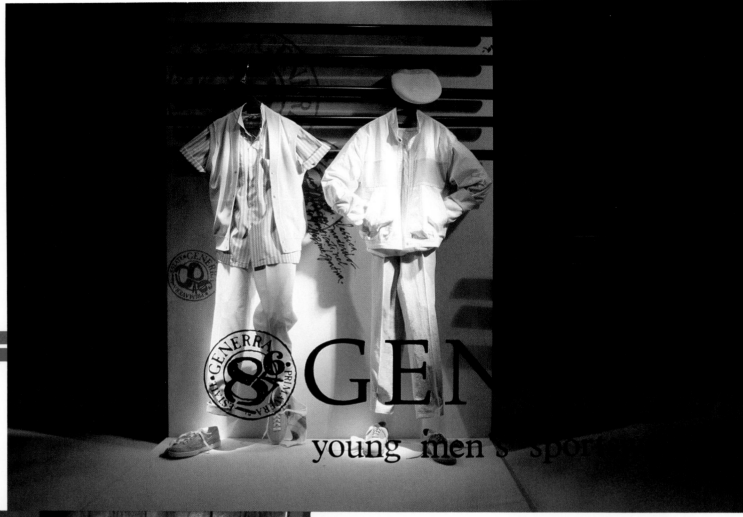

A mannequin-less display utilizes PVC pipe, mounted on fabric panels, to display merchandise. The black logo on the window coordinates with the pipe.

A display of subdued sophistication was created for the Calvin Klein display in the Men's department.

A cement-finished column, platform, and table are accented with neon to highlight the new "International News" selection. The popular T.V. video is visible on top of the scene.

The S.F. Bay Athletics logo was created by the in-house Visual Merchandising department for apparel that includes men's and ladie's active apparel and shoes. The logo is also screened on the merchandise.

Activewear is displayed with the illusion of motion with athletically-posed mannequins. The black background highlights the bright colors of the merchandise.

Outerwear in the Generra shop is creatively displayed on fabric panels. The 6-foot tall mannequin-less display utilizes PVC pipe.

The "San Francisco Bay Company" line was displayed on grids created with PVC pipes and Seven Continents Italian Clamps, and accented with neon. It makes an interesting contrast with the casual clothes.

The Juniors "Street Chic" statement display includes simulated cement panels, black pipe and counter balance forms.

A display of subdued sophistication was created for the Calvin Klein display. The natural wood panels — made in Emporium-Capwell's production center — form a perfect backdrop for the brown-toned clothing. The mannequins are by Pucci.

A Southwest theme merchandises casual clothing in natural tones. Background lighting simulates a sunset.

SOUTHWEST PASSAGE

ROBERT BENZIO

Saks Fifth Avenue, *New York, New York*

Robert Benzio is presently Senior Vice-President, Director of Visual Merchandising at Saks Fifth Avenue. He is totally immersed in all of the store's visual merchandising presentations, including interior and window displays. He has imprinted his stamp on many of the Saks around the country, as he has been involved in twenty new stores during the past eight years of his tenure.

Benzio's extraordinarily successful career in Visual Merchandising started twenty-six years ago. His first position was as a display trainee at Franklin Simon. His talent proved valuable, as he rose to Senior Director at B. Altman & Company in a relatively short period of time.

Benzio left B. Altman's in 1968 to joint DePinna as Display Director. From 1969 – 1971, he worked at Best & Company in a similar position. Benzio applied his growing talents in display design on a freelance basis for a year before rejoining B. Altman, this time as Display Director.

Robert Benzio has received an impressive amount of recognition as one of the finest Visual Merchandisers in the business. He first gained notoriety in 1973, when he was named *Visual Merchandising's* Display Man of the Year. He then received the National Association of Display Industries (NADI) Annual Display Award, both in 1973 and 1974. *Inspiration*, a display trade publication based in Switzerland, granted Benzio admission to their Academy of Inspiration in 1976.

The National Association of Display Industries had no trouble naming Robert Benzio a member of their Hall of Fame in 1978.

Though unprecedented, it came as no surprise when Benzio received the NADI's Annual Display Award for 1982 — for the third time! He was also awarded the Fine Arts Award.

Benzio was most recently honored by NRMA in 1984, when he was named Visual Merchandiser of the Year. Later that year, he became one of the first three people chosen to receive the Society of Visual Merchandisers Accreditation. This honor entitles him to use the respected initials, SVM, after his name.

Benzio's work is typified by simplicity. He rarely uses an abundance of props; the merchandise is always the most vibrant element of the display. He thoughtfully selects accessories — such as jewelry, simple shoes or hats, and lipstick — in colors which highlight the featured clothing. Displays are always well-lit, and, with rare exception, against a light background which further stresses the merchandise.

Benzio's displays contain a few simple, yet dramatic props which usually echo the color of the merchandise. The excellent results are highlighted by expertly placed lighting.

A pair of trees and a reclining male figure, stippled with
subdued colors, form the dreamlike background for the
wardrobed mannequin. She becomes part of the scene
while remaining distinctly the main attraction of it.

The vibrant hues pulled from the latest swimwear and
leotard fashions form a connecting path between the two
mannequins, appropriately suggesting fluidity and motion.

▶

In this window, Benzio employs props to lend an oriental ambiance. The graceful evening wear is a natural part of the setting.

The large picture mirror enables passers-by to view all sides of the shimmering cocktail dress at once with a quick glance.

Customers are invited into Sak's Ungaro display by an unobstructed view of a sampling of his latest designs. The plush beige carpeting doesn't interfere with the hues of the fashions. Well-lit recessed racks encourage browsing.

The elegance and comfort of this shimmering gown are a part of the mannequin's world, as she rests her arm on a plush pile of pillows.

Benzio invites intrigue with this simple scene that makes a statement — passers-by view the bride in all her splendor, then wonder why the extra chair is propped against the wall.

This provocative window display demands attention. The seated woman doesn't seem worried, as her muscle-rippled arm illustrates what can be accomplished while donning the latest workout-wear.

Mannequins attired in colorful spring loungewear are staged in the casual setting of television-watching amid undone gardening chores.

The classic styles and colors of the Valentino line are clearly the focal point of this display. Benzio has allowed a generous amount of space around the racks for admiring the designs individually. The traditional character of the clothing is restated by the no-nonsense white, black, and brass color scheme. A pair of narrow black stripes run around the top of the walls, unifying the Valentino section of the store.

The elegant black and white dresses steal the scene in contrast to the pale mannequins. A few wisps of red lipstick and jewelry are the only brightening elements.

A well-selected prop helps set the mood; the
long-legged, aristocratic Afgan hound is the perfect
complement to the graceful, flowing lines of the evening
gown.

Benzio features his often-used black and magenta color combination, this time, to spotlight patterned stockings and simple, almost masculine clothing.

The gaily patterned, loose fitting clothing is echoed by the billowing flag overhead. The fabric is highlighted by the pair of solid-colored hats. ▶

CHAPTER 3

LINDA BRAMLAGE

Miller & Rhoads, *Boston, Massachusetts*

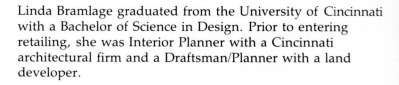

Linda Bramlage graduated from the University of Cincinnati with a Bachelor of Science in Design. Prior to entering retailing, she was Interior Planner with a Cincinnati architectural firm and a Draftsman/Planner with a land developer.

Bramlage started her Visual Merchandising career in 1972 with Shillitos in Cincinnati. In 1978, she joined Meier & Frank in Oregon as Visual Merchandise Manager, then relocated to Richmond, Virginia where she joined Allied Stores Corporation's Miller and Rhoads as Associate Visual Merchandise Director. She was later promoted to Director of Visual Merchandising, and then Vice President, Director of Visual Merchandising.

In March of 1985, Bramlage was appointed to her present position, Vice President/Director, Corporate Visual Merchandising of the Jordan Marsh, New England stores.

Bramlage's display work shows particular attention to merchandising themes, whether classically elegant, contemporary, or even African in nature.

Bold, imaginative selections of props and
accessories create dynamic settings which enhance
the merchandise.

Lightweight, casual summer fashions are arranged in a tropical-style setting. The abundance of brightly colored fruits on the table adds contrast to the cool pastels of the clothing.
Designed for Miller+Rhoads.

The casual, brilliantly colored winter fashions are smartly displayed against a neutral background. Mannequins enforce the feeling of "excitement" for the clothing. Designed for Jordan Marsh.

The entrance to the exclusive "Virginia Room" is flanked by a pair of seductively posed, glass encased mannequins. The gold lettering on the cases reinforces the theme of elegance.
Designed for Miller+Rhoads.

The popular designs by Perry Ellis are comfortably arranged in an estate-like setting of delicate trees and heavy cement railings. Since the clothing is of different styles and fabrics, the mannequins are spaced apart.
Designed for Miller+Rhoads.

A charming holiday display features the traditional
red and white color scheme on display tables and
columns. Highlights of gold add sparkle to the
giftware. The foreground figure greets customers
and adds character.
Designed for Miller+Rhoads.

Tableware is arranged in an African-style setting of
greenery, zebra tablecloths, and sarong-skirted
black statues. It is in sharp contrast with the china,
making the samples seem extra-elegant.
Designed for Miller+Rhoads.

The varied shapes, sizes and colors of the pottery, china and glassware are accented, using black display cubes with white-colored tops. The mirrored wall panels highlight the merchandise with the help of overhead lights. Designed for Jordan Marsh.

Frilly pillows, comforters and sheets create a soft, romantic look for this fine linens department. Pink, rose-patterned fabric adds just a touch of color. Designed for Jordan Marsh.

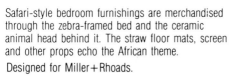

Safari-style bedroom furnishings are merchandised through the zebra-framed bed and the ceramic animal head behind it. The straw floor mats, screen and other props echo the African theme.
Designed for Miller+Rhoads.

From the mall's entrance, a view of both the housewares and domestics departments are clearly visible. A natural wood-color floor separates the individual departments. Floor material varies within these departments, complementing the decor of each. Designed for Jordan Marsh.

The contemporary clothing is reinforced by the artful selection and arrangement of props. The checkerboard floor and black and white sculptures mime a game board. Even the arrangement of the mannequins is sharply symmetrical.
Designed for Miller+Rhoads.

Unusually-hued men's shirts need no other props but good arrangement and color grouping. Neatly arranged racks placed right at the aisle entice customers.
Designed for Miller+Rhoads.

Elaborate pedestals, dramatically arranged, present shoes in an elegant fashion.

Casually posed mannequins in glass encased displays present a contemporary look for Perry Ellis. Accents of white contrast with the otherwise shadowy background. Designed for Jordan Marsh.

FRANK C. CALISE

Bonwit Teller, *New York, New York*

Frank Calise emerged from the backstage of a New York theater 25 years ago. Louis Viella, then the display director for W & J Sloane, had seen Goethe's "Iphegenia in Tauris," and was so impressed by set designer Frank Calise's work that he asked him to join his staff.

Currently Vice President of Visual Merchandising at Bonwit Teller, New York, Calise has spent the past quarter century spreading his talents through an array of the finest stores in the United States.

His stay at W & J Sloane from 1960 – 1963 offered him a new way to showcase his creativity. Designing furniture displays seemed like theater to him, and his ideas were constantly challenged. Viella taught Calise to look at things in a different way, sometimes turning his sketches upside down — literally. As a result, he learned never to do the obvious or trendy.

Calise moved on to Bloomingdale's in 1963, where he set up departments and created tablesettings in home furnishings. He soon made an easy transition to ready-to-wear displays.

On a self-imposed exploration, Calise left Bloomingdale's and the New York area in 1973. He joined Cain-Sloan of Nashville, Tennessee, as Director of Visual Marketing. After a year and a half, Calise moved on to Jordan Marsh in Miami, Florida, where he was named Vice President. He remained there until 1978, when he went on to Miller & Rhoads of Richmond, Virginia, again as Vice President, Director of Visual Marketing.

Calise was enticed back to New York in 1980, for the exciting planning of Bonwit Teller's reopening in the newly constructed, palatial Trump Tower. He now directs a staff of 36 in the store planning department, branches, and sign shop. Calise provides creative direction for all window and interior displays, and is quick to credit his staff for their inspired implementation.

Calise acknowledges that visual merchandisers have to "forget ego." First and foremost, they have to be aware of what is right for the company and its customers. The thrust is on the bottom line — retailers are in business to sell merchandise.

Among numerous awards and recognitions, highlights of Frank Calise's career include NRMA's Visual Merchandiser of the Year for 1985, and the Visual Merchandising Award for 1978 (Large Store Category) from NADI (National Association of Display Industries).

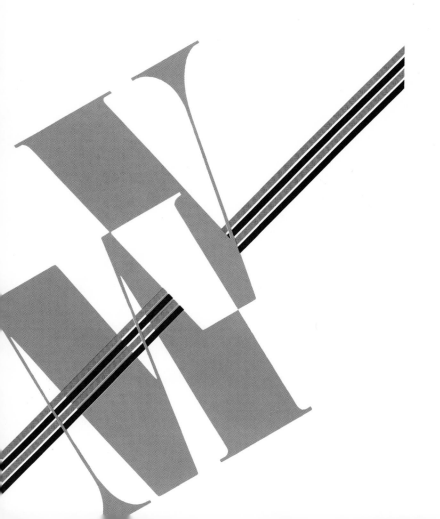

Calise invents creative ways to merchandise a single theme throughout every department store.

This dramatic Christmas window is a beautiful sight from the cold winter street. The tiny white lights of the tree help illuminate this scene of casually placed Christmas gifts.

Calise has expertly put together a store window of feminine Christmas gifts. The contrasting colors play beautifully off of each other against a background of a single huge wreath of evergreen and bows.

Neon-bright clothing literally stands on its own: the striking colors and patterns playfully mix together on the wire grid; other designs are grouped together as they may daringly be worn.

Here the mannequin shows off, in a carefully arranged tumble, Christmas purchases from the Men's shop. Already-wrapped gifts reinforce the spirit.

A white athlete statue highlights the dress through both its color and position.

Suspended in the "iron cross" position, this pair of athletes form interesting images that may be viewed from many angles.

A gymnast twirls above a display of hand-embroidered handkerchiefs.

A feminine figure gracefully arches over the cosmetics section.

The all-American teddy bear poses to promote the
Olympic theme with a T-shirt and "Wheaties" cereal.

A promotional aid for the "American Express" card
becomes part of the star-spangled "America" theme.

Red, white and blue sportswear on this pair of mannequins subtly conforms to the "Celebrate America" theme.

A pure red pole vaulter dons on Olympic-like uniform to introduce the clothing in the Athletics department.

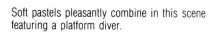

Soft pastels pleasantly combine in this scene featuring a platform diver.

This oversized painting of a gymnast in mid-air is flanked, on top and bottom, with live greenery.

Yet another sports scene focuses on a swimmer who's ready for a rest break.

A diver in action is set off by a huge palm tree on the right.

JOSEPH FECZKO

Duty Free Shoppers Group Limited, *San Francisco, California*

Joseph Paul Feczko is Corporate Director of Visual Merchandising for the Duty Free Shoppers Group Limited. This international retail organization currently owns and operates over 120 stores. Mr. Feczko's responsibilities include merchandise presentation, store planning and fixture designs, packaging, product development, seasonal decor, signage and graphics.

Feczko works magic with colors, frequently putting together dramatic monochromatic displays, or expertly coordinating colors to create a mood. Whatever the color scheme, the merchandise is always the focal point, and it is often supported by careful arrangement among theme-enhancing props.

Feczko is a native New Yorker and a graduate of New York University. Prior to his current position, he was Vice President, Visual Merchandising for Federated Department Stores' Burdine's in Miami, Florida. He was also Executive Secretary, Federated Department Stores Visual Directors Committee (FDVC). Feczko has also held a position as Vice President, Director of Visual Merchandising at Joske's, Dallas, Texas, which is an Allied Department Store.

Mr. Feczko is an active board member with the National Retail Merchants Association. He has won numerous design awards, most notably Best Store Design — 1984 from National Association of Display Industries (NADI).

Props become an integral part of the scene in many of Feczko's merchandise displays. Combined with effective placements of the mannequins, the mood is instantly relayed.

Sheer lingerie is romantically displayed among
huge baskets of baby's breath. The soft white and
beige tones create a soothing image.

Colors highlight each other in this expert
combination of lingerie. The sofa adds to the mood
while adding its shiny black complement.

The legs of a woman become the legs of a table in this unique hosiery display. Colors playfully work together to humorously enhance the merchandise.

A row of evergreens decorated in red and white beautifully stand out from the usual white background. The red is picked up on appropriate areas of the display cases.

Repeating images of floral arrangements and the "in bloom" poster seem even more dramatic on the long, comparatively narrow aisle. Rows of small lights on the ceiling strengthen the image of the posters.

The huge atrium in the West Palm Beach store is dominated by a billboard-sized collage. The predominant white background, warmed by the neutral floors, is appropriate to the warm weather setting.

This display is reminiscent of a black and white print, as no bright colors intrude on the scene. Even the mannequins are gray. Spot and flood lights highlight the merchandise while creating interesting shadows.

Movement and action are used to promote men's casual clothing. Even the necktie is carefully arranged to seem frozen in air.

Designs by Guess are fashionably coordinated on the hangers. The patterns on top of the poles are encased in Guess' signature shape, the triangle.

A flower promotion is creatively enhanced by the coordinating clothing of the mannequin. The contrasting texture aids in showing off their varying shapes and textures.

A glamorously attired couple catch the attention of passers-by in this store window. The flamboyant woman's headpiece is the focal point, as it is fully illuminated in the spotlight. The subtle hues of the shadows are an enchanting background.

Classically designed swimwear is displayed in a tropical setting of bamboo and greenery. Each of the three mannequins is wearing the same multi-colored necklace, which shows off the bold color of each suit.

A pretty spring outfit with the classic wide-brimmed hat support the garden theme of the flower promotion.

A provocative display of sheets shows the patterns
swaddling mannequins, as their coordinates are
more traditionally arranged alongside them.

Contemporary bed and bath accessories are aptly arranged on a stark modern display. The many textures and patterns of the same color combinations creatively show off the coordinates.

A comical representation of a chef, merchandises housewares in front of an antique icebox.

The entrance to the Generra shop shows a trio of mannequins in coordinating separates. The clear lucite board behind them displays the designer's logo, while maintaining openness and allowing customers to see the shop's merchandise.

Sweaters in the Polo shop are complemented by the multi-hued Indian rug. The well-lit back wall shows off the neatly folded coordinates.

Clothing for young men is coordinated and repeated for effect on both mannequins. The uniform look is reinforced by the popular image of musicians.

THOMAS JEWELL

J.C. Penney Company, Inc., *New York, New York*

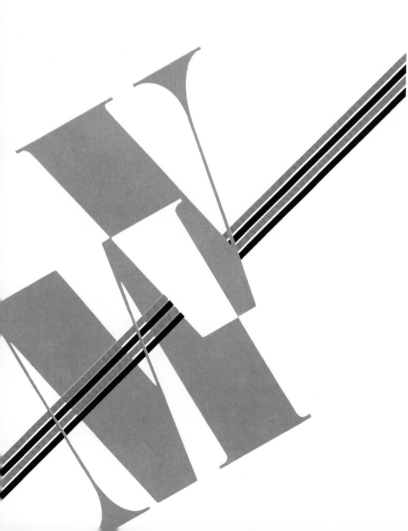

Thomas R. Jewell, presently Manager of Corporate Marketing projects for J.C. Penney Company, Inc., feels that visual merchandising is the single most important element of retailing today. He points out that since most stores are in malls, they don't have store windows as they did in the past. He feels that the retailer should make a visual statement by presenting excellent displays that will catch the customer's attention immediately. He explains that the merchandise among competitors is so similar, the retailer that presents it best — through lighting, fixtures, and merchandising — will be most successful. Jewell refers to his style as "romancing the merchandise," and, like many other successful visual merchandisers, calls his art "theatre."

Jewell was J.C. Penny Company's first Manager of Visual Merchandising. He efficiently pulled together the related responsibilities of merchandise development, packaging and labeling. He has been Manager of Corporate Marketing Projects since early 1984, an assignment that includes coordination of J.C. Penney Company's Classic Mixed Team Golf Championship and the JCPenny/United States Clay Courts Tennis Championship, as well as their "Best of Britain" and "Salute to Italy" promotions. Jewell is a longtime associate of the company, having started his career with them in 1966 as a sales and merchandise manager in Youngstown, Ohio.

Jewell is currently on NRMA's Visual Merchandising Board of Directors. He is also on the board for *Chain Store Age Executives*.

Featured items at J.C. Penney are displayed on custom-designed fixtures that are specifically sized for the merchandise.

Featured loungewear is dramatically presented beneath a dropped octagonal ceiling section. The ceiling is echoed by a flooring change, from tile to carpeting.

An enormous, provocative poster helps guide customers to the Lingerie department. The mirrored feature wall beneath it aids in creating a feeling of openness.

Fashion shots make mood-creating posters in the Junior department. The interesting construction serves to display merchandise on mannequins as well as on sales racks.

Several sizes of triangles are positioned to simulate three figures modelling the featured fashions. The paint is color-coordinated with the rest of the department.

This designer feature display in an attractive color scheme employs an interesting stepped platform; a glass display attached, shows suggested accessories.

Featured merchandise is highlighted by presentation on fixtures that blend with the floor color. These units are specifically sized for the particular merchandise. This plan allows the merchandise to boldly stand out from its nearly invisible background.

A pink gloss laminate wall and an interesting light fixture attract attention to the featured merchandise in the Shoe department. Wall posters identify the type of merchandise around them, helping to guide customers. Stepped display units also highlight a large, varied amount of styles. The special mirrors allow viewers to see themselves from head to toe.

Clear glass shelving adds an interesting element to the bath accessories display. The items graduate from dark on the bottom to light on the uppermost shelves. Color gradations are also present in the towel displays.

Home Furnishings coordinates are expertly arranged in adjoining alcoves. Well-placed lighting adds drama to the scenes.

An interesting tile pattern, a changed ceiling level, and masculine light fixtures combine to create the illusion of a separate shop for Men's Furnishings. Small impulse items are smartly placed in an interesting arrangement on the aisle.

The eye is led to the young men's display by neat, symmetrical racks of merchandise. The theme of hubcaps is used in the display and on the walls. Intriguing posters decorate the central back wall area.

A quietly elegant menswear display features clothing on an antique-style pine sideboard. Added masculine elements include the decoy, hairbrush and attaché. Beautiful, traditionally styled lighting completes the setting.

Customers can't miss the ''Sesame Street'' children's line, as a bright logo and large Muppet figures are clearly positioned all around the merchandise. The sales racks contain both forward- and side- facing merchandise, assisting in the self-service process.

The feature walls in the ''Big Kids'' section are defined by a creative ''jungle gym'' grid in bright orange. The lighting is attached, adding visual interest as well as illumination. The impact of the feature wall is increased by changing the way garments are presented: they front hang on the feature wall, and shoulder hang on the back wall.

Implied containment creates a huge shopping focal point in the Men's Furnishings and Accessories department. The ceiling is raised two feet above the standard ten foot area surrounding it. This height change is directly above an attractive flooring change. Displays have been placed to accentuate the geometric floor pattern. This interesting sub-section is topped off by good lighting.

Featured merchandise is presented on fixtures that blend with the floor color. These units are specifically sized for the particular merchandise. This plan allows the merchandise to boldly stand out in the aisle.

ROBERT MAHONEY

Gump's, *San Francisco, California*

Robert J. Mahoney, Director of Display at Gumps, has been with the store for twenty-five years.

It should come as no surprise to those familiar with his work to learn that Mahoney has a background in theatre, having previously been Technical Director for Actor's Workshop.

The displays at Gumps are very dramatic. The key, according to Mahoney, is simplicity, with basic white windows - except at Christmastime. Mahoney frequently uses "negative space" as part of the design. He has been greatly influenced by Oriental design, which is a big part of Gumps' history.

Mahoney "sets the stage" for his dramatic displays, which are often influenced by Oriental design.

"A tribute to Italy" was merchandised through a dramatic arrangement of masks and flowers. They're perfectly highlighted by the exact placement of the spotlight, resulting in interesting shadows.

A TRIBUTE TO ITALY

A mood was established for the Italy promotion with the olive wreath and authentic-looking section of a column. They serve as a background to the merchandise, featuring a fuchsia cape and a metallic purse. The draped fabric alongside the purse matches the mannequin's outfit; her gold belt accents the purse.

One-of-a-kind treasures were presented through a museum-style setting, complete with protective glass cases and exacting lighting.

Wall hangings are presented in a museum-like style, with plenty of room around the art for unobstructed inspection. The neat border of yellow flowers adds a unifying element and color that ties all of the pieces together.

Unique wall hangings are presented in a museum-like style, with plenty of space around the art for unobstructed, clear inspection. The neat rows of gold flowers which border the wall add a unifying element as well as color that ties all of the pieces together.

An array of fine dining accessories along the walls are set off by the impressive feature presentation. The elaborate chandelier crowns a beautifully coordinated table of crystal, china, and accessories.

Christmas cards were promoted through a wintery
scene that inspires customers to "inquire within."

The Christmas circus theme was highlighted by individual circus animal displays, captioned with a holiday greeting in a multitude of languages.

The Christmas circus theme was highlighted by individual circus animal displays, captioned with a holiday greeting in a multitude of languages.

A circus environment was created to surround the Christmas tree. The tree displays Gump's ornaments, which are casually grouped below in wicker baskets along with other decorative accessories.

A simple but dramatic arrangement captures the elegance of the fine Danish dinnerware. The blue and white display is fully illuminated, with halos of light encircling the three place settings.

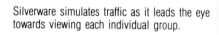

Silverware simulates traffic as it leads the eye towards viewing each individual group.

Exquisite tapestries form an enclosure for the pretty dining scene. Bright gold flowers highlight the blue and white featured merchandise.

A narrow blue runway visually pulls together the display of humanlike planters. The designer's signature forms a decorative border.

An unusual statue posed with a chrysanthemum-bordered reflecting pool is the focal point for an extensive line of blue and white china. Coordinating pieces are shown on adjoining tables, as well as on an elegantly appointed blue and white tiled table in the foreground.

FROM GUMP'S BERRY PATCH.

A charming little tree forms the perfect perch for berry-decorated china "from Gump's Berry patch." The scroll's lettering coordinates with this whimsical scene.

Glassware and ceramics were displayed in this courtyard setting surrounded by Ionic columns and marble statues.

PRESENTING
Spanish Baroque

REED & BARTON STERLING
6-PIECE PLACE SETTING
57⁰⁰

"Spanish Baroque" silverware is neatly suspended in mid-air, framed by a pair of similarly designed columns. The scroll-like sign completes the mood.

Marble Ionic columns supporting a Roman frieze, as well as sections of marble flooring, were selected as the setting for giftware in the Italy promotion. Track lights were carefully placed to dramatize the props and highlight the featured merchandise.

Unique blue and white china figurines are neatly arranged on the white-topped tables with highlights of bright yellow chrysanthemums.

A tented ceiling creates the flavor of an international market in this section of the gift department. An abundance of unusual merchandise is invitingly arranged, allowing the customer to see many items at once, among image-enhancing counterparts.

Display props of well-known British decorative elements set the stage for an Irish stone sculpture. Lighting is positioned to best highlight the sculpture's features.

A play on words promotes the "$\frac{1}{4}$ off sale" with a line-up of four bowls that had one-quarter of each removed.

Cement dog sculptures are lined up at the fire hydrant. This necessary height change prevents complete flatness of the display.

Gump's welcome to "Friends of the American Concrete Institute" was merchandised through whimsical cement sculptures.

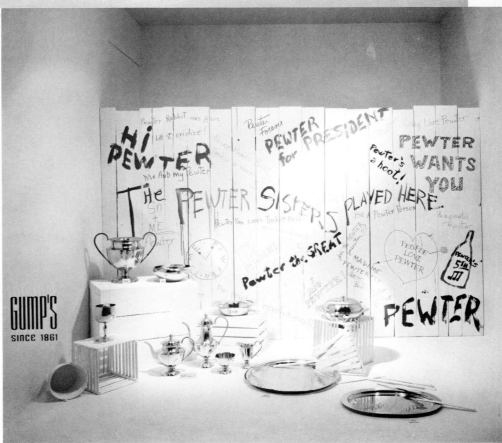

Fine pewter giftware is backed by a humorous graffiti-covered fence.

Decorative "Hakata Dolls" are staged in a minimalistic setting that is characteristic of the Japanese. Their colorful costumes and action poses attract undivided attention.

Oriental figures form the backdrop for a small sculpture of a monkey.

A perched peacock, with a humorous caption, introduces a variety of decorative eggs.

Decorative oriental eggs are grouped in real eggs cartons. Their obvious differences from the real thing, however, are noted in the balloons.

Beautiful trays, composed of pressed leaves and flowers, are characteristically presented through their association with a scrapbook. The calligraphy on the scroll before it identifies it to the Italy promotion.

Hollywood-style lights invite a closer look at the merchandise. Arranged in nests, the eggs are captioned with their suggested uses.

A small display humorously merchandises the pure white swan dish. Carefully arranged gold rope "hair" leads the eye to the well-lit focal point.

Crystal animals are presented on flat hand stages
to merchandise the "Hand Coolers" theme.

Unusual wood boxes are shown in a
three-dimensional setting with their drab corrugated
counterparts.

A Turkish style of lettering identifies the origins of the copper pieces. The colors are accented, and the merchandise pulled together, by the Turkish-designed fabric arranged like a tent.

RABBITS LOOKING AT THE MOON 30.00 each

Along with the casually scrawled "From Gump's, San Francisco," the metal sculptures of familiar area scenes resembles picture postcards.

In a scene from an Oriental story, rabbit sculptures are presented in a well-arranged scene.

Stepped sizes of beautifully shaped fine china bowls are dramatically arranged and expertly illuminated against an unusual background arrangement. The lettering resembles miniature bulb lights.

A pair of cartoon elephants seem to stumble among a precarious arrangement of stemware. Their balloon captions, and those of the mouse, describe the details of the sale.

Crystal ashtrays are merchandised through the use of layers of golden circular blades. Along with the pitch black background, it offers a stage that complements the facets.

A beautifully detailed vase, washed with light, contains a haunting illusion of flowers in a rainbow of colors.

An elegant vase is dramatized with a mysterious floral arrangement.

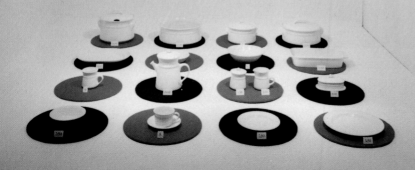

Casual, white dinnerware stands out on the graphic arrangement of blue and gold discs.

The red plate helps to merchandise china, in an interesting play-on-words.

A cutlery sale is merchandised through a gleaming stainless steel display. Carefully placed lights form interesting highlights.

A single clock design becomes more powerful by its varied repetition. The gold tones are highlighted by the identifying lettering.

Plastic stemwear is artfully arranged on gears. Upon closer inspection, one may read the price information on the gears. The foreground glassware and lunchbox introduce the theme.

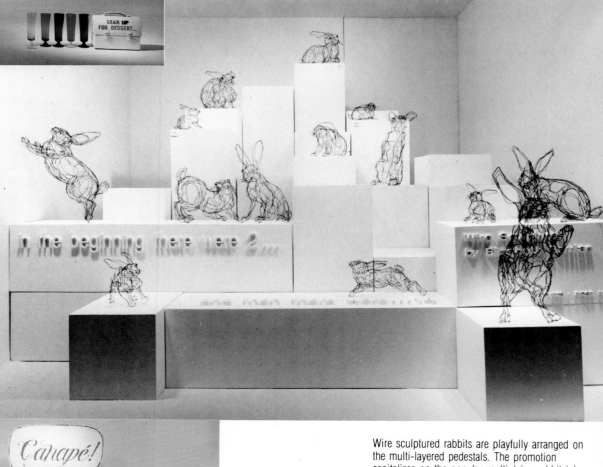

Wire sculptured rabbits are playfully arranged on the multi-layered pedestals. The promotion capitalizes on the popular multiplying rabbit joke.

The cheerleaders' rhyme promotes the neat line-up of gold canape trays.

The suspended salad ingredients ingeniously add splashes of color and also balance the copy in this display window.

The casually styled tableware is identified by Western-style signage that sets a mood and highlights the designer's name through color. Spotlights bathe the merchandise with pools of light.

A fleet of copper sailboats are promoted in a creatively-designed ocean. The flags balance the scene and provide the details on the merchandise.

A pair of twisting vines form an interesting framework for the elegant silver bowl.

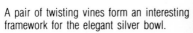

A ceramic camel statue is presented in a setting that remarkably resembles the camel's natural habitat. Lighting creates a pseudo-sun and shadows that make the free-standing letters easier to read.

A brass horse is presented in a rugged, outdoors-like setting with huge blocks of stone.

Glassware and trays decorated with roadrunners are arranged with a frenzied scramble of lifelike roadrunners. Naturally, the line made famous by cartoons is included.

RICK MCCLELLAND

Jordan Marsh Florida,   *Miami, Florida*

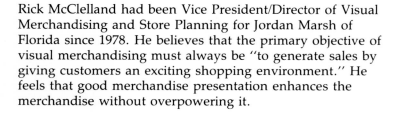

Rick McClelland had been Vice President/Director of Visual Merchandising and Store Planning for Jordan Marsh of Florida since 1978. He believes that the primary objective of visual merchandising must always be "to generate sales by giving customers an exciting shopping environment." He feels that good merchandise presentation enhances the merchandise without overpowering it.

McClelland's career started in 1968, when he was employed as a part-time Men's trimmer of Titche's (now Joske's) in Dallas, while he was attending Southern Methodist University. He soon rose to Branch Manager, then Assistant Director, then Director of Visual Merchandising. He spent a year as Visual Merchandising Director for Gimbels in Pittsburgh before moving to his present position at Jordan Marsh.

McClelland often blends elements of humor and surprise into otherwise conventional displays. For example, children's clothes are displayed on "mannequins" resembling oversized flat, stuffed dolls; a cartoon character becomes part of a linen display. McClelland also dramatizes merchandise by presenting it before a specially designed background, be it water for swimwear or cartoon frames for playful casual clothing.

McClelland was recipient of the Second Grand Award in *Visual Merchandising* Magazine's International Display Competition in both 1981 and 1982.

McClelland's merchandise displays frequently incorporate elements of surprise . . . the customer can't help but take a second look.

Three styles of women's suits are portrayed on a
trio of mannequins, lined up as identically posed
singers. The vertical white lines of the microphone
stands highlight the dark hues of the merchandise.

A pure white seagull, framed by a cracked egg, is the perfect setting for the deep violet shell jewelry.

Customers' attention is immediately drawn to the shiny red sportscar amidst Better Dresses. The foreground rack shows off a coordinating red and white outfit, and closer inspection reveals an elegantly-attired female mechanic at work beneath the car.

An array of accessories are expertly coordinated on a single mannequin. The narrow mirror panels in the background reinforce the contemporary image.

Bedding coordinates are displayed in a creative setting with a covered wagon and sun-bleached wood. The passenger, a huge stuffed "Wile E. Coyote" adds a humorous element.

Men's activewear is theatrically presented by a pair of mannequins in an ancient-looking vessel strewn with fishnets and . . . a mermaid!

A swimming pool was created through the use of tiles and a mural of rippling blue water, forming a spot where Men's Swimwear is shown off.

The wall of the Men's Active Shop is highlighted by a palm tree motif along the top edge of the wall. It is broken by the bright "Greetings from Florida" poster above the bicycle-riding mannequin, a scene that sets the mood for the sporty array of merchandise.

The Coca-Cola Shop's clothing is so graphic, good arrangement on racks is the best way to highlight the merchandise. These racks and parts of the light fixture mountings are constructed of a rough-looking, factory-like material. The ceiling subtly contains a few panels of the company's familiar logo.

Men's contemporary sportswear is positioned on mannequins that are backed by a pair of pillars and neon star outlines.

THOMAS NATALINI

Allied Stores Corporation, *New York, New York*

As Corporate Director of Allied Stores, Tom Natalini says he is fortunate to be working with an outstanding Store Planning and Design Division. He feels that good, clean design, good departmental adjacencies and good lighting form the basis for creating visual merchandising "theatre" related to each department.

He prefers to sell merchandise without clutter, through unobstructed departments and good display presentation. Natalini strongly believes that the right fixtures must be selected — or created in-house — to attract the customer's attention.

He then adds the design elements that match a department's personality. Natalini stresses that proper lighting is vital to the presentation, making a weak area become a strong one.

Natalini must have an open mind to each of Allied's diversified units, as design direction must be in keeping with each company's individual identity.

Many of Natalini's displays use repeating images to form a strong display theme for all sorts of merchandise. In this type of setting, the merchandise is clearly the focal point.

Classic china is presented in a classic setting of pure white pedestals, clear glass and polished silver. Oversized floral arrangements help balance the scene while adding to the luxury.

The repetitive patterns of the tables draw the viewers' attention down the aisle. Housewares are arranged on the aisle's perimeter.

The colorful stripes of the towel wall are the background for a lineup of towel-draped mannequins.

The Safari-themed bedding by designer Perry Ellis is casually layered upon the beds and highlighted by solid-colored pillows.

A group of white-clothed mannequins create interest above the elevator well. White pedestals hold vases of arrangements that complement the flooring.

Lights abound to highlight the variety of styles available in the Dress department. A raised platform, trimmed in brass, exhibits three samples.

The terrazzo floor delineates the pathway between the sub-departments of Juniors. The displays are tied together through the use of neon.

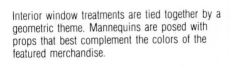

Interior window treatments are tied together by a geometric theme. Mannequins are posed with props that best complement the colors of the featured merchandise.

A kickline of legs exhibits the huge line of hosiery. Similar styles are grouped together to capitalize on the repetitive image. A row of fish-eye lights spotlights the merchandise.

Strands of pearls are presented in their element: an underwater scene. The grey stones of the fish and scuba diver accentuate the lustrous white of the jewelry.

Men's belts are comically displayed on a long row of white torsos, animated by bow ties and red boutonnieres.

The Better Sportswear department is characterized
by a clear display of an abundance of
merchandise. Most notable is the use of the
recessed white background for the outward-facing
wall racks, clearly standing out from the gray-green
tones carried out in the rest of the section.

The featured outfit is repeated three times: as an outfit of coordinates on a pair of mannequins, then separated and mounted on the foreground. A row of bright gold mums adds a splash of color.

The contemporary theme of the "Junior Exchange" is merchandised through the clean, simple lines of the glass display case and highlights of pink neon throughout. The identifying sign is visually framed by the pair of umbrella-wielding mannequins.

Interior window treatments are tied together by a geometric theme. Mannequins are posed with props that best complement the colors of the featured merchandise.

RONALD NELSON

Z.C.M.I., *Salt Lake City, Utah*

Ron Nelson is Corporate Director of Visual Merchandising at Z.C.M.I., having climbed the ladder through all of the positions in the visual merchandising department.

Nelson received the Annual Display Award for Outstanding Achievements in 1979 by the National Association of Display Industries. He was elected to their Hall of Fame in 1985. Nelson has also been recognized by Visual Merchandising's International Display Competition for winning the First Place Award for seven consecutive years.

Nelson is a member of the Inspiration Academy.

He has contributed to various trade publications, as well as the Whitney Library of Design's "American Store Window," by Leonard S. Marcus.

Visual displays at Z.C.M.I. are dramatic, creative, and theatrical . . . sure to attract the customer's observation!

Bold art artifacts demand attention while they complement the color and style of the featured clothing. Designed by Mike Stephens.

The severity of the black and white outfits is both accented and softened by the interesting color-splashed sculpture. Designed by Mike Stephens and Jutta Gellersen.

A huge bust helps to merchandise the Italian clothing. The mannequins are perfectly arranged so that the sculpture, as well as the clothing, is readily viewed from many different angles of approach. Designed by Diane Call.

"Italy holds the fashion world captive at needle's point"

Dhurrie rugs are suspended in mid-air, showing their beautiful colors and patterns to full advantage. Plants placed on lucite pedestals before them also seem to float. Designed by Sheldon Trimble.

A lone black leather sofa sits stage center as an expertly-arranged gust of photographs freezes in midair flight. Designed by Dennis Wardle.

A nearly symmetrical modern furniture arrangement glares from the nearly monochromatic walls and floors. This cold setting allows each piece to stand on its own merits. Designed by Dennis Wardle.

A well-arranged disarray focuses upon the merchandise in the center. Its contrasts to the background and illumination is reminiscent of a beautifully dressed person amidst a cluttered dressing room. Designed by Jutta Gellersen.

White, black and gray subtly blend as the literal spotlight is on the unusual footwear. Designed by Jutta Gellersen.

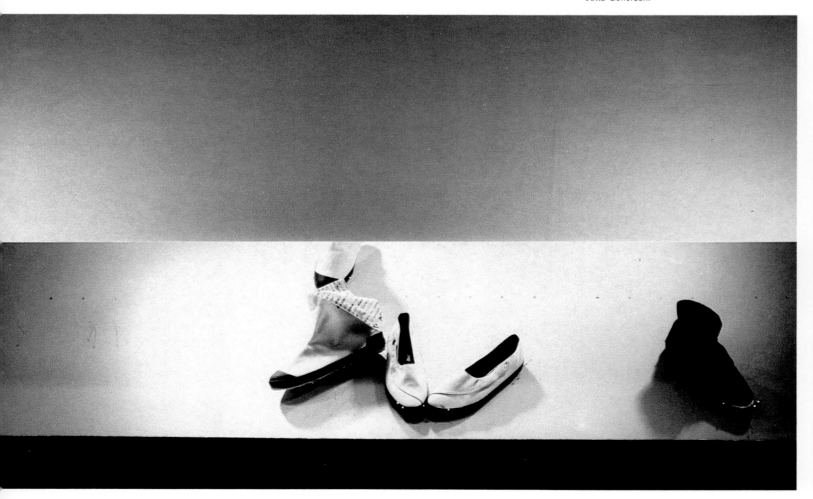

Beautiful belts are simply yet elegantly arranged on geometric shapes, highlighting the softness of their construction. The statement "For the Waist" helps pull the concept together. Designed by Sheldon Trimble.

The oddly unbalanced chair and the play on words draw attention to the merchandise. Lighting enhances the image. Designed by Diane Call.

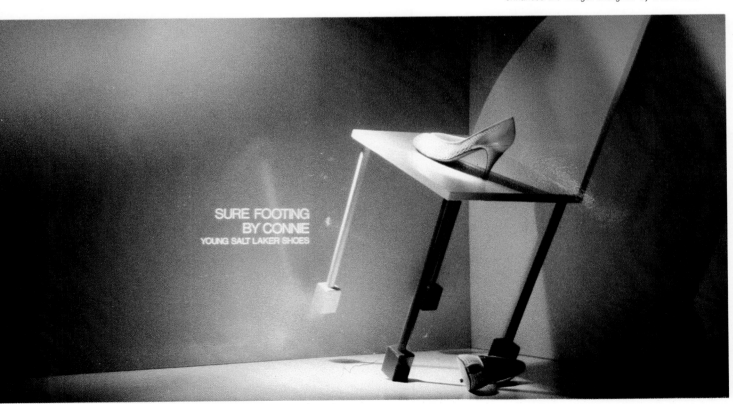

Luxurious flowers beautified the Mother's Day
window. Designed by Diane Call.

This window display for the Glassware department uses simple elements to create an elegant and striking picture. Designed by Maureen Miller.

A theatrically staged window promoted the ''Live!'' theme. Designed by Mike Stephens.

The pure, bright colors of the oversized shirts are emphasized through their contrast to the platform. The simple screen prop helps frame the mannequin and doesn't compete for attention. Designed by Dennis Wardle.

The stylishly attired mannequins are framed by a creatively structured three-dimensional rectangle which picks up the colors in the wardrobe and the accompanying caption. Designed by Dennis Wardle.

Colorful sportswear is presented in a simple white platform setting, set off by bare poles. Designed by Mike Stephens.

Pure white geese become part of this winter merchandise scene. Their beautifully arranged flight enhances the lush evergreens and glamorously dressed mannequins. The small white deer similarly add whimsical interest. Designed by Mike Stephens.

This eye-catching display dramatizes cloth hampers in a rainbow of colors. The soldier-like row is enlivened by the color arrangement and the headline letters. The display is accented by expertly arranged white cloths flying around the white corner. Designed by Sheldon Trimble.

Colors and repeating images merchandise the white sale goods. In the foreground, prints coordinate with the solid colors behind them, enhancing both. Designed by Dennis Wardle.

Stepped cylindrical platforms hold merchandise for "The Graduating Class." Designed by Terry Stephens.

A grouping pf pleasant pastel colors promotes some of the merchandise available during the "White Sale." Designed by Dennis Wardle.

Giftware is beautifully arranged as a shop in itself. Creative use of the white pedestals allows interesting viewing of many items at once in one small area. Colors have also been thoughtfully chosen to play off of each other. Designed by Jutta Gellersen.

Glass-encased merchandise is highlighted by red banners. Designed by Dennis Wardle.

An interesting reversal of colors is an ideal accent for undecorated china in black and white. The red and white striped napery and solid red and white tables play beautifully off of each other. Designed by Anne Cook.

GIFT GALLERY

Bold flowers and umbrellas enliven the arrangement at the Gift Gallery. Otherwise invisible glass vases are put to attractive use while they become more prominent. Designed by Jutta Gellersen and Anne Cook

An attractive spring wardrobe is beautifully presented among the vibrantly hued flowers; pink umbrellas create a roof for the display. Designed by Mike Stephens.

A grouping of glass-topped tables is enhanced by well-planned floral arrangements. Designed by Anne Cook.

Fashions for men are dramatically set in an Italian scene. The pillar constructions and background painting sharply contrast with the modern, dark colored styles. Some pillars have been knocked down to display merchandise. Designed by Mike Stephens.

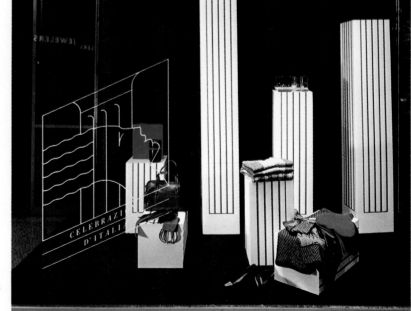

Representations of pillars serve as pedestals for merchandise in an Italian promotion. The displays color scheme of black and white with highlights of red heightens the drama. Designed by Mike Stephens.

The logotype for the "Celebrazione D'Italia" promotion is a see-through foreground for the featured merchandise. A painting in the background reflects the Italian influence. Designed by Brian Smith.

The wintertime department entrance is enhanced by an abundance of evergreens and tiny white deer statues. The glamorously attired mannequins are a beautiful part of the scenery. Designed by Mike Stephens.

Marble tables are laden with giftware and silver in
this lavish Christmas window. Designed by Dennis
Wardle and Anne Cook.

A mixture of ceramics form the display for the two designer lines. Designed by Sheldon Trimble.

Colors and squares are artistically combined to highlight a series of mugs by Marimekko. Their checked patterns are echoed by the tiles they're placed upon, with a pair of ceramic tile strips behind them coordinating with the merchandise color. The display is well lit to aid in the reflection of the products. Designed by Donna Matthews.

This arrangement of "Color Classics" beautifully displays giftware. Designed by Anne Cook and Robin Stepps.

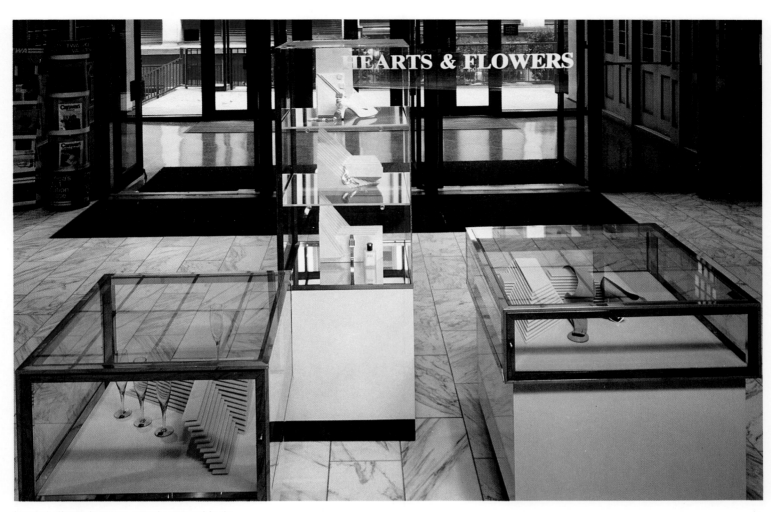

Assorted giftware items are expertly arranged in the "Hearts and Flowers" section. Designed by Fritz Schultz.

A suspended white cloth flutters beside an elegant red crystal bowl. Designed by Maureen Miller.

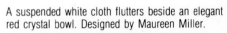

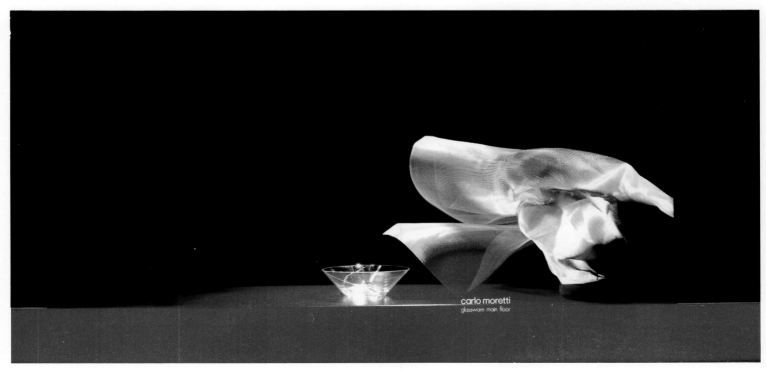

An Italian theme is promoted though the abundance of columns in this display on the women's fashion aisle. Designed by Mike Stephens.

A warm weather outfit is simply presented with greenery in the foreground. The green ladders are reminiscent of a trellis, and help frame the mannequin. Designed by Dennis Wardle.

The "Flower Market" is merchandised with a spring wardrobe on the mannequin amidst a lovely arrangement of flowers.

An elegant gray-veined marble floor is the backdrop to the housewares section. Simple black tables serve as pedestals while they coordinate with the repeating promotional symbol in black, red, and white. Designed by Anne Cook.

A "Mountain Time" theme is an inventive way to merchandise an array of casual clothing. Designed by Eric Stephenson.

Interesting shadows are formed by the poles, while they help to frame the "Summer Picks" wardrobed mannequins. Designed by Brian Smith.

Transluscent black fabric is interestingly gathered to frame the casually dressed mannequin; the mixed-type headline labels the "transitional" theme. Designed by Sheldon Trimble.

ANGELA PATTERSON

Bergdorf Goodman, *New York, New York,*

Angela Patterson is currently Vice-President and Director of Visual Presentations at Bergdorf Goodman in New York, where she has been working since 1981.

Patterson started her career at Dayton Hudson in Minneapolis, Minnesota as a Display Staff Member. She then moved on to Pogues in Cincinnati, Ohio where she worked as Assistant Display Director.

Later, Patterson worked at Hahne's in New Jersey as Display Director, advancing to Divisional Vice-President of Visual Presentations.

Display windows at Bergdorf Goodman attract the attention of passing New Yorkers with dramatic contemporary settings. A few simple, well-selected props create an instant mood.

Men's and women's eveningwear by Gianfranco are
displayed through the combined use of
mannequins, two-dimensional forms, and soft
display.

Mannequins donned cartoon-like masks in this
unusual introduction to the designs of Jean Paul
Gaultier. The window artwork by artist Laurie
Rosenwald represents various neighborhoods in
New York City.

The Issey Miyake Shop on the first floor of Bergdorf-Goodman is dominated by Mr. Miyake's interpretation of Coca-Cola bottles. The terazzo blocks containing chips of the broken glass cover the walls, floor, and columns. The back wall is illuminated from behind by fluorescent lights that penetrate through the glass particles.

These traditionally styled gowns are presented in a stark contemporary setting created with well-placed candles and fishnet.

The outlined print of Christmas trees on the window are juxtaposed to ten foot tall real trees on Fifth Avenue.

Unusual chalk-skinned mannequins were used to display couture evening clothes by Yves Saint Laurent. Theatrical arrangement of the draperies guide the eye to the merchandise.

For the first time at Bergdorf's the display windows featured a symbol that furnished information relating to sale merchandise and the location of departments . . . instead of merchandise!

Featured clothing is presented on a conveyor belt, reflecting designer Issey Miyake's love of contemporary automation and movement.

ALAN PETERSEN

John Wanamaker, *Philadelphia, Pennsylvania*

Alan Petersen is currently Vice President, Visual Merchandising for John Wanamaker, Philadelphia, a division of Carter Hawley Hale Stores. He had previously held various buying and merchandising responsibilities at the Broadway, Southern California branch (another Carter Hawley Hale division) including Director and then Vice President of Visual Merchandising.

Petersen is skilled at theme presentations. He always creates a variety of interesting merchandising approaches, and the resulting displays generally reflect a clean, contemporary style.

Petersen was recipient of the National Association of Display Industries Award in 1974. He is a member of the Retail Advisory Committee for the Western Association of Visual Merchandisers, the Divisional Merchandising Board of Directors for the NRMA, and the Institute of Store Planners.

Petersen's skill at theme presentations reflect a creative and interesting approach to merchandise display.

John Wanamaker's traditional "Light Show" is a huge, breathtaking display high above the main floor. The ledge presentation of tiny white lights adds to the festivity without detracting from the main attraction.

The new line of Coca-Cola clothes is displayed through a high-tech theme and the predominance of the company's familiar logo.

The neon Coca-Cola is the crown of the department's entryway. Videos behind it form the backdrop and frame for a simulated stage.

The gift department was highlighted by a collection of flags from the Region of Tuscany. Their predominant colorings of red, black, and white are coordinated by the fixtures, displays, and carpeting.

"The Market on Market" entrance is highlighted by an Italian farm cart and large white umbrellas with tivoli lights. A red, green, and white color theme predominates.

The contemporary stationery and gift department, "Milan Today," is notable by its striking presentation of black, white, and yellow merchandise artfully arranged on gleaming black pedestals. The salmon-hued background highlights the colors of the merchandise; the added masks make it a dramatic poster.

The aisle is dominated by a 38-foot long Venetian gondola — imported from Venice — with hand carved wood decorations.

Four clothing display racks are carefully arranged to frame the three figures in formation with the promotional video. A repeating Coca-Cola logo identifies the department.

This display combines the promotions for men's swimwear with the storewide Walt Disney promotion.

A bicycling theme was selected for the decoration of the Men's Active Shop during the Italian Renaissance promotion. The neon wheels add a dramatic contemporary touch.

A Pinocchio theme charms the Children's clothing shop. Colorful wooden figures pose with the display mannequins, and a repeating image highlights the ceiling lines. Pinocchio's long nose became a pole on which to hang merchandise.

The store's Walt Disney promotion starred Mickey Mouse (and friends) in every available merchandising space.

A huge Donald Duck became a surprising part of the women's clothing display as part of the Walt Disney promotion. Even the mannequins casually don Mickey Mouse headwear.

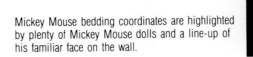

Mickey Mouse bedding coordinates are highlighted by plenty of Mickey Mouse dolls and a line-up of his familiar face on the wall.

The cashmere sweater shop display features mural-sized sepia enlargements of Venice on the back walls. The foreground's black mannequins in black-rimmed glass cases draws attention to the merchandise, while emphasizing the subtle tones of the background.

A cluster of mannequins displays original Missoni-designed costumes for the La Scala production of Lucia di Lammermoor.

The Coca-Cola shop's back wall features illuminated posters of fashion shots. The lighting is positioned so that a double image is created by the logo which is screened on a transparent material. The central mannequins show how loose and comfortable the clothing is designed to be.

JOSEPH POWERS

Bamberger's, *Newark, New Jersey*

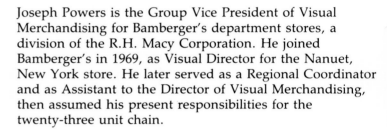

Joseph Powers is the Group Vice President of Visual Merchandising for Bamberger's department stores, a division of the R.H. Macy Corporation. He joined Bamberger's in 1969, as Visual Director for the Nanuet, New York store. He later served as a Regional Coordinator and as Assistant to the Director of Visual Merchandising, then assumed his present responsibilities for the twenty-three unit chain.

Among many other skills, Powers makes use of the often-unused merchandising space on walls. He creates dynamic displays that feature the merchandise, often using repetitive images for effect. He may also mount lettering or posters on the walls. These displays serve a dual purpose by helping guide customers to their selections as well as by highlighting merchandise.

On other displays, he often dramatizes the merchandise with a few well-selected props or by effectively combining colors in an interesting fashion.

Powers' interest in the field started at the Fashion Institute of Technology in New York, where he majored in Fashion Illustration.

He currently resides in Princeton, New Jersey, where he is a board member of the Historical Society, and is active in the preservation and history of local architecture.

Effective combinations of colors and patterns with minimal props, create an appropriate mood for the merchandise that is unique to each department.

A dramatic effect is achieved by repeating the same image. The trio of dark-skinned mannequins show off the gleaming pearl jewelry. Bunches of ribbon-tied evergreen sprigs create a holiday look, and baby's breathe further highlights the pearls.

Fine Jewelry is displayed on oversized photographs behind the cases, alleviating the problem of showing items that are too small and valuable to be placed out in the open. There is plenty of room around each of the "islands" for customers to look into the cases; sales people can also see who needs attention.

The Anne Klein II section is dramatically
introduced by a single mannequin, her striking
clothing clearly the hot spot of an otherwise
unoccupied living room. Coordinates are clearly
displayed as a background to the mannequin.

Three mannequins model styles in an outstanding
three-tiered display fixture. Their outfits coordinate
through colors and accessories. Other merchandise
in the "Attitudes" department are shown in
outward facing racks along the wall.

The colorful array of clothing in the Expressions department is subtly accessorized by black and white graphic elements. Plenty of space around the sections allows the customer to glimpse many of the styles at once.

The latest fashions are shown in combination on the pedestaled mannequin, as reference to the coordinating styles displayed on glossy black bars. The high-tech feeling is also reflected by the abundance of chrome, glass, and mirrors.

A quartet of mannequins display designer Calvin Klein's outerwear. They are thoughtfully positioned to show off each coat's features; for example, the cape is comfortably draped on the reclining mannequin. The color theme of black and red is accentuated by coordinating accessories. A white stage and sculpture serve as an appropriate backdrop.

Lightweight outerwear is featured in a
warm-weather setting. Bamboo posts and a
tropical-style plant arrangement are highlighted by
casually draped pink fabrics and pastel clothing.

The chunky letters in the "Kenzo" display window echo
the bulky, layered style of the clothing. The letters seem
to be just-arranged, with spare blocks serving to balance
the scene.

The dramatic white lace and silky black evening dresses play off of each other, contrasting the attractive features of each. A huge bouquet adds accents of color and glamour.

Elegant glass cases and mirrored columns feature the designers in the Lingerie department. Flowers and graceful bird statues complete the look.

Stylishly attired mannequins arranged on dramatic black props introduce the Signature department. The featured designers are clearly listed beyond them, making shopping easier.

The large Junior Perspective department in Bamberger's Monmouth store is unified through the geometric elements of the columns, and the blue neon striping along the walls which echo the "Perspective" identifier. Several similar-looking mannequins introduce the area at the entrance points.

"Clubhouse Classics" are dramatized by the graceful layers of black and white clothing on the pair of mannequins. Their festive appeal is touted through the beautiful evergreen flower arrangement.

Attractive signage for the Expression department attracts attention with the unique cut-outs for light. Above the sign, a pair of mannequins playfully illustrate the fashions. The sphere between them is replayed with slight variations along the walls and in other areas of the department.

Unusual gold palm props become the unifying motif for the Signature's Shop. The window display features representative designs, creatively reversing colors on each mannequin, using gold, black and white. A center island picks up the gold on a sweater,. Mirrored columns become nearly invisible while allowing customers a viewing of many of the fashions within.

Free-standing white lettering identifies the designer while picking up the accent colors in the suit.

The Children's and Teen's departments are noted by playful geometric shapes in bright primary colors on the walls and mannequin platforms. These elements are a contrast to the black ceilings and pure white mannequins.

An enormous variety of shoes are arranged for the Signature Shoe department. Noted designers and their line are displayed in individually framed wall sections. More merchandise is shown on stepped platforms, leaving nothing out of sight.

The designers featured in Junior Perspective are identified by easy-to-read lettering mounted high on the wall. This method simulates the creation of departments within a department, and customers can easily crossover.

The luxury of the Lingerie department is reflected in the soft taupe of the walls and carpeting. Floodlights are used to highlight garments on the wall and on the glass-encased mannequins.

The polo theme of designer Ralph Lauren's line is reinforced by the props used in playing the game. This enhances the perceived exclusivity of the clothing.

Powers' well-designed focal column serves more than one purpose. It identifies the department with the brass lettering, and exhibits the clothes through the backlit photograph of a model and grid-mounted body mannequins.

The distinctive logo of Polo by Ralph Lauren classifies the garments viewed beyond the masculine wood-framed glass in the Livingston store.

The Ralph Lauren department, with antique-like furniture, resembles an old-fashioned shop. The oversized baskets of gold flowers, tied with red and green ribbon, highlight the colors of the beautiful sweaters.

The entrance to the Young Men's department is flanked by flat-topped mannequins posed against neon tubes. The patterned carpet complements the styles within.

An unusually creative wall display attracts attention to the Loft & Brownstone polo shirt line. The yellow arms wielding racquetball racquets accentuate the bright colors and the circles contrast with the stripe patterns.

A strong wall presentation of Rugby shirts and
Soccer balls was designed for Bamberger's King of
Prussia store. The black and white Soccer balls
help add contrast to the vibrant colors and designs
of the shirts. Repetition strengthens the theme.

The traditional designs of the private label "Charter
Club" line are displayed in a club-like setting of
polished wood, a big wing chair and a simple
plaid area rug.

Special fixtures show off fashions on polished chrome bars against a black background. The image is repeated several times, resulting in a well-organized contemporary design.

A small display window holds the "Charter Club" logo and merchandise display, setting the department off as a shop within the store.

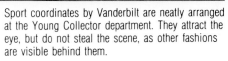

Sport coordinates by Vanderbilt are neatly arranged at the Young Collector department. They attract the eye, but do not steal the scene, as other fashions are visible behind them.

The classic designs of the private label "Charter Club" are displayed in a subdued fashion, with the flowers, lighting, and plaid carpeting eliciting a country-club atmosphere. The timelessness is further enhanced through the use of the old-fashioned wooden shelving along the back wall.

Ski wear is promoted in its natural setting — on skiers. The white "snow" highlights the bold colors of the clothing.

The expansive Children's department is broken down into sections by the white ceramic tile path amidst the green carpeting. Videos provide entertainment while supporting clear lucite panels, which are screened with sub-department identifiers.

Children's hard goods are beautifully displayed in a rainbow of primary colors. Care has been taken to perpetuate the dazzling color patterns, with similarly colored items grouped together. The department is introduced by a childlike poster and even a red mannequin garbed in bright clothing.

Bed linens are glamorously displayed on a canopied pine bed. The bedroom look is accessorized by the blanket rack, free-standing mirror, and large shuttered window. The simulated view of the cold outdoors emphasizes the warmth of the merchandise.

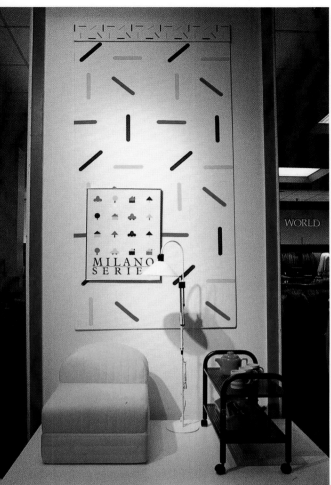

This vignette in the ''Habitat'' hardgoods section spotlights a simple and clean focus on the merchandise. The stark graphics and primary colors are picked up on the backdrop pattern and poster.

The high-tech Electronics department is merchandised by an unusual red mannequin, with top hat and cane, alongside video equipment. Passersby can't help but notice the display . . . especially when their own face appears on screen! The screen is enhanced by the surrounding grid pattern.

Glamorous black lace holiday dresses are featured
in a Christmas window. Their drama is accented by
the pale mannequins and appropriate jewelry —
right down to an ankle bracelet.

A festive table setting, and a much-too-proper
butler cut-out is an elegant display for this
Livingston, New Jersey store.

The entry to "The Cellar" section of the store displays the type of goods that might be expected within. A hostess-attired cow stands at a table of foods, tableware and giftware . . . in the holiday spirit with a country-style Christmas tree.

This colorful Christmas scene features
gaily-dressed jesters amidst a Christmas wreath
with gold ornaments.

The homey entryway to the Country Kitchen department gives a glimpse of the items within through the holiday red-white-and-green color scheme.

Christmas decorations are appealingly arranged in a chest and around the tree in a cute, cosy cottage style setting.

STEVE RIX

Maas Brothers, *Tampa, Florida*

Steven C. Rix is Senior Vice President, Visual Merchandising and Store Planning for Maas Brothers, a division of Allied Stores Corporation. The store's merchandise displays clearly focus on the merchandise, with a few complementary accessories or props.

Rix entered the visual merchandising field with F.R. Lazarus Co. in Columbus, Ohio in 1964. In 1973 he became Display Director for their branch stores.

Rix joined Maas Brothers in 1973 as Assistant Visual Merchandising Director. He became Vice President, Visual Merchandising and Store Planning in 1978 and in 1984 was promoted to his present position.

Contemporary-styled geometrics and bold, integral accessories of many merchandise displays designed by Rix.

A silver background provides the glamour and reflection for this attractive display of women's accessories. Gold in the scarves, jewelry, and belts is the unifying element.

Pure white mannequins permit the merchandise to be the star. Christmas packages at their feet add a subtle suggestion.

Geometrically shaped blocks combine to form a stage for men's sportswear. Lighting creates interesting shadows that emphasize the shapes.

Giant scallop shells provide subtle lighting and a simulated headboard while bringing out the colors in the bedspread.

The "Little Luxuries" sign identifies the department while allowing customers to see right through it. The reclining mannequin before it, on a creatively designed platform, adds the suggestion of relaxation.

The popular "Miami Vice" television series attracts the same young men that the featured clothing styles do. Unusual mannequins emphasize the contemporary look. The arrangement of branches mimes the triangles.

JAMES SEIGLER

Foley's, *Houston, Texas*

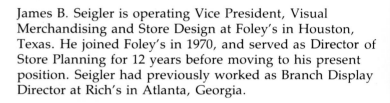

James B. Seigler is operating Vice President, Visual Merchandising and Store Design at Foley's in Houston, Texas. He joined Foley's in 1970, and served as Director of Store Planning for 12 years before moving to his present position. Seigler had previously worked as Branch Display Director at Rich's in Atlanta, Georgia.

Seigler believes that "Visual design and store design should only be used as a means to enhance the merchandise that is for sale. It should be used to create an ambiance and an environment in which the customer would feel comfortable and stimulated."

He adds, "A store should be a continuous stage or theatre in which the merchandise is the actor. It is the one element of retailing left that can make one store or shop look and feel different than the one across the street."

Seigler is a member of NRMA's Visual Merchandising Board of Directors, and has spoken at NRMA seminars. He is also a member of the Retail Advisory Committee of the West Coast Association of Visual Merchandisers. He is a charter member of the Society of Visual Merchandisers, and is on the Accreditation Board for this group.

Seigler serves on the Steering Committee for Federated Building Executives and as a sponsor for their subcommittee on Interior Planning and Design.

Seigler was awarded the National Association of Display Industries' citation for outstanding contribution to the industry as a creative store planner in 1979 and 1983.

Seigler's merchandise displays clearly serve as a means to enhance the merchandise. The settings usually focus on highlighting particular colors or patterns.

Foley's Christmas windows featured five beautiful scenes inspired by the nearby Houston Ballet's annual seasonal performance.

Designer clothing for men is presented in a no-nonsense setting with polished woods and neutral wall colors.

The simple background of white with black pinstripes and scattered geometric shapes sets off the daring graphics of the "Swatch" line.

Athleticwear makes a statement as a parade of mannequins step up the bright red display. Their soldier-like form and identically styled outfits create excitement through repetition. The foreground figure is positioned to balance the scene.

The bright hues of the boys' running suits seem even brighter against the rich red background. The suggestion of movement is emphasized by their identical positions.

The Children's department is playfully decorated with a parade of circus elephants. The elephants are topped with mannequins wearing featured children's fashions that everyone is sure to notice.

"Baby it's cold outside" . . . the message gets across with icicles, snowflakes, and a trio of Santa-capped mice. The merchandise is appealingly arranged in mesh grid boxes.

Shirts featuring cartoon characters are a display in themselves. The oversized filmstrip and video-headed mannequins reinforce the comic theme.

A colorful combination of clothing is highlighted by the solid geometric shapes behind them. The mirror allows the customer an interesting view from all approaches.

Subdued colors magically blend together to create a pleasing display of sweaters and coordinates. The face-out racks make this a self-service display.

Elements from the gleaming black and white floor are picked up and dramatically arranged on the back wall. The featured design is displayed on an elegant pedestal table.

Multi-tiered platforms are adorned with mannequins all wearing black evening wear. This piece is an attractive center store display and can be seen from all levels.

HOMER SHARP

Marshall Field's, *Chicago, Illinois*

Homer Sharp, Vice President of Design at Marshall Fields, has been with the store since 1946. He started in the display department, moved on to Manager of Interior Display in 1955, and then Display Director in 1968. In 1970, store design was added to his responsibilities. In 1971 he was promoted to his present position.

Mr. Sharp, a native of Cleveland, Ohio, was educated at the Parsons School of Design and at the Mid-West School of Art and American Academy of Art in Chicago.

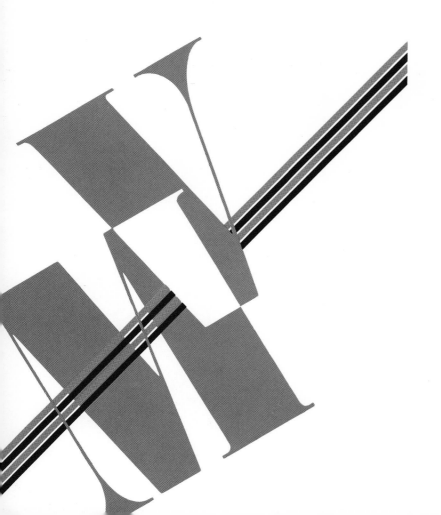

Visual displays at Marshall Field's are on a grand scale, sparing no expense to create a beautiful shopping environment.

CHAPTER
17

R. KENNINGTON SPIKES

Cain-Sloan, *Nashville, Tennessee*

Ken Spikes has held the position of Director of Visual Merchandising, Store Planning with the Cain-Sloan Company since 1975. Cain-Sloan is the Nashville, Tennessee division of the Allied Stores Corporation, which is headquartered in New York City.

Spikes started his career in the display business in 1961, as a display trimmer with Rich's Atlanta. Under the guidance of Dudley Pope, he was given the opportunity to participate in every phase of visual endeavors. He became Display Manager of the Store of Homes, then Branch Store Display Manager, and finally Director for all branch stores, nine at that time.

In 1975, Spikes accepted his present position at Cain-Sloan. At that time, department stores were rapidly moving from what was known as "display" into the new and expanded world of "Visual Presentation." His creative ability, high taste level, and directional sense have earned him a highly respected status in the company. Spikes' involvement is not limited to visual functions, going deep into the areas of special events and advertising as well. Spikes possesses a particular strength in the Home area, and is a member of the buying team at the High Point furniture market.

Spikes uses three basic rules in visual merchandising: 1) Let the merchandise be the star — don't overpower it with props, 2) Do something provocative to catch the eye, and 3) Above all, make sure every presentation is tastefully executed.

Ken Spike's talent has earned him recognition on the Board of Directors of the NRMA Visual Merchandising Division. His advice and talents are frequently sought after by local museums, theatres, the Country Music Hall of Fame and the performing arts.

Spikes received the coveted NADI Annual Display Award for 1978. His most recent recognition was the induction as a permanent member into the exclusive Society of Visual Merchandisers.

Spikes's humorously "plays on words" with merchandise displays. He capitalizes on a given charactersitic or brand name by building upon it with a unique setting.

Young men's sportswear coordinates are exhibited
in an updated style without the use of mannequins.

Store-brand sportswear, "Crew" is illustrated through the scene of a construction crew. Spotlights highlight the mannequins.

Men's winter outerwear is appealingly arranged in a wooded setting, complete with an antique sleigh.

Women's separates are dramatically modeled by sharply posed mannequins. They're neatly balanced around the contemporary sculpture, which was constructred in-house.

Sets of point-of-sale make-up brushes are shown on a foam core artist's palette. Packages are beautifully grouped according to color.

The neon-hued fashions for Juniors is presented beneath the eye-catching MTV.

A play-on-words was created for "Jellies" brand shoes. The array of colorful merchandise stands out on Styrofoam representations of toast.

ROBERT UNGER

Burdine's,   *Miami, Florida*

Robert Unger has been working at Burdine's in Miami, Florida as Vice-President of Visual Merchandising and Store Design since November 1984.

Prior to Burdine's, Unger worked at Saks Fifth Avenue of New York in Personnel. He then worked in Personnel in Bamberger's where he later acquired the position as Regional in Visual Merchandising. From Bamberger's, Unger joined Jordan Marsh of Boston where he was Vice-President of Visual Presentations.

Unger served on the Board of Directors for NRMA and WAVM.

In 1983, Unger received the Annual Display Award from the National Association of Display Designers for outstanding achievement in his field.

Unger enjoys highlighting merchandise through color. Subdued backgrounds form an almost invisible stage.

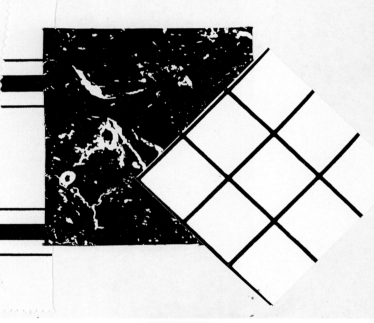

Bold, contemporary graphics feature a playful mix of black and white patterns.

In contrast to the bold, contemporary style of the columns and flooring, the mannequin is subtly framed with color through the three red strips on one side and yellow background of the signs on the other.

The tropical colors and patterns of this casual clothing highlight the Children's department .

Burdine's "Mix It" shopping bag graphically merchandises the theme through varied patterns and surprising colors. The lettering for "Mix It" is a mixture of typestyles.

Colorful and patterned footwear stands out on white pedestals in a variety of shapes and heights. A strand of neon leads the eye through the center of the display.

A display for the ''Mix It'' theme contains a mixture of white patterns and textures. The vibrant blocks of color add visual interest.

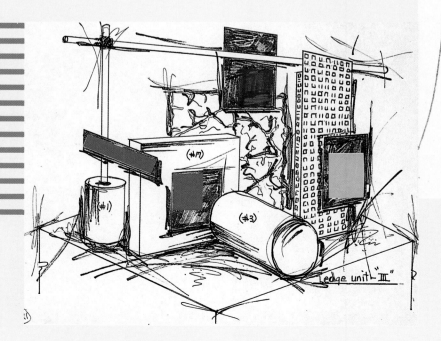

Display plans are mapped out by detailed sketches splashed with color.

A play-on-words, "Fit to be tied," shows off boldly colored neckties against a subtly-hued background. A nearby display of clothing color-coordinates with the ties.

The "color with black" theme features black and white clothing with bright highlights of color. Burdine's basic white background is the perfect stage.

Boldly colored bedding coordinates are casually strewn about the unusual four-posted bed. The colors are picked up by many of the props, which serve to balance the light background scene.

The escalator rises up to the atrium atmosphere of the open-walled second floor. The Christmas trees add color, sparkle and atmosphere — especially in contrast to the palm tree columns.

A display of brightly-colored clothing is enlivened for Christmas by loads of tiny white lights, cascading in a loosely-structured curtain.

The "In hot pursuit" theme features brightly-colored merchandise in each department. This angle shows its Christmas-time connection through the evergreen decorations at the end of the long aisle.

White flamingo statues merchandise the hot colors
of the feature promotion with an interesting
arrangement of colorful ribbons. The mannequin
draws the eye with a T-shaped pose in a black
jacket.

18-17
A menswear display gets a Christmas touch with
the bold placement of giant evergreen wreaths. In
the same spirit, the mannequins are clothed in
Christmas colors.

CHAPTER
19

ANDREW J. MARKOPOULOS

Dayton Hudson, *Minneapolis, Minnesota*

Andrew J. Markopoulos is currently exercising his extensive knowledge of Visual Merchandising techniques in the position of Vice President of Visual Merchandising at Dayton Hudson, of Minneapolis, Minnesota.

Prior to Dayton's, Markopoulos was Vice President and Director of Visual Merchandising for Gimbels' Philadelphia store. While there, he left his mark through his commanding involvement with the "Market East" design team that searched the world for furniture, artifacts, and contemporary pieces. This successful program added a unique ambiance of warmth, elegance, and art flavor to Gimbels.

His impressive roster of achievements most notably includes membership in the prestigious and exclusive "Inspiration Academy," a worldwide organization that has only granted membership to three other people in the United States at present. Markopoulos has also been awarded "Outstanding Visual Merchandising Management" by the National Association of Display Industries.

Markopoulous applied his Visual Merchandising expertise in a unique way by creating the decor for the dressing rooms of the Walnut Theatre for the historic Carter-Ford debate.

He shares his knowledge of Visual Merchandising through frequent lectures at Drexel University. Markopoulos is also a popular speaker at NRMA Visual Merchandising and Design Seminars, as well as many workshop and consultation sessions.

Markopoulos creatively displays
merchandise, adding warmth,
elegance, excitement and art
flavor to Dayton Hudson.

An exquisite chandelier adds a touch of elegance to the Cosmetics department.

Soft pinks and beiges create a warm, feminine quality for this display of Estée Lauder. The decorative flowers and poster reinforce this feeling.

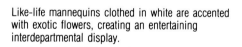

Like-life mannequins clothed in white are accented with exotic flowers, creating an entertaining interdepartmental display.

The use of white and black create a clean look for this clothing department. Life-like mannequins sport the casual attire.

The use of green and tan create a natural setting for the Boundary Waters display. Sweater-garbed mannequins, naturally colored baskets, pictures and horses enforce an "outdoorsy" atmosphere.

Casually clothed mannequins introduce the Juniors department. Shiny silver balls add a sense of festivity to the scene.

Mannequins bundled up in wintery attire are strategically placed before the entrance to the River Room Restaurant.

The richly-colored Oriental tapestry and red Oriental poppies create an ambiance of sophistication for these designer shoes.

"Target practice" is the startling theme for these mannequins dressed in red and black outerwear, sure to catch the attention of all passersby.

Candy is elegantly displayed against a white background with gold-colored flooring, with a mannequin dressed in formal wear to attract the attention of passersby.

Mannequins are strategically placed along the aisle, modeling the clothing found in their respective departments.

Fluorescent-colored merchandise is highlighted against a dark background. Spotlights pick up the metallics, creating a sense of "electricity" in the air for the Electronics department.

China and glassware is elegantly displayed against a subdued background. Rose-colored flowers and lampshades add a hint of color to the department.

A very formal, dark setting, with crystal chandelier and red roses, is created to display fine crystal.

An assortment of china and glassware is casually arranged, with mauve and copper-colored accents.

A variety of merchandise for Ralph Lauren is stylishly displayed in a natural, wood setting.

Flower arrangements are artfully displayed, relaying the image of "Pastoral Romance."

Colorful woolens are deliberately arranged among brass-colored objects. The bulky, wooden furniture creates a very masculine setting.

1. NRMAS's Visual Merchandising Board of Directors

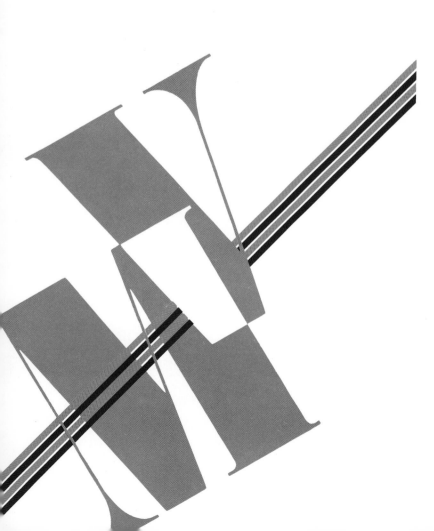

Thomas Azzarello
Vice-President, Visual Presentation
Emporium-Capwell
San Francisco, California

Robert Benzio, svm
Senior Vice-President, Corporate Visual Merchandising
Saks Fifth Avenue
New York, New York

Cecil Bessellieu, svm
Corporate Visual Merchandising Director
Belk Stores Services
Charlotte, North Carolina

Linda Bramlage
Vice-President, Visual Merchandising
Miller & Rhoads
Boston, Massachusetts

Frank C. Calise, svm
Vice-President, Visual Merchandising
Bonwit Teller
New York, New York

Joseph Feczko
Operating Vice-President
Duty Free Shoppers Group
San Francisco, California

Thomas Jewell
Manager, Corporate Marketing for Geographic Markets
J.C. Penney Company, Inc.
New York, New York

Robert Mahoney
Director of Display
Gump's
San Francisco, California

Andrew J. Markopoulos, svm
Vice-President, Visual Merchandising and Design
Dayton Hudson
Minneapolis, Minnesota

Rick McClelland
Vice-President, Director of Visual Merchandising
Jordan Marsh Florida
Miami, Florida

Lilian Matthews McNiff
Vice-President, Corporate Merchandise Presentation
Dayton Hudson
Detroit, Michigan

Thomas Natalini, svm
Corporate Director, Visual Merchandising
Allied Stores Corp.
New York, New York

Ronald Nelson
Display Manager
Z.C.M.I.
Salt Lake City, Utah

Angela Patterson
Vice-President, Director of Visual Presentation
Bergdorf Goodman
New York, New York

Alan Petersen
Divisional Vice-President, Visual Merchandising
John Wanamaker
Philadelphia, Pennsylvania

Joseph Powers
Group Vice-President
Bamberger's
Newark, New Jersey

Steve Rix
Vice-President, Visual Merchandising and Store Planning
Maas Brothers
Tampa, Florida

James Seigler, svm
Operating Vice-President, Visual Merchandising and Store Design
Foley's
Houston, Texas

Homer Sharp
Vice-President, Design Division
Marshall Field's
Chicago, Illinois

Thomas Speedling, svm
Senior Visual Merchandising Specialist
Navy Resale & Services Support Offices
Staten Island, New York

R. Kennington Spikes
Vice-President, Visual Merchandising
Cain-Sloan Company
Nashville, Tennessee

Robert Unger
Vice-President, Visual Merchandising
Burdine's
Miami, Florida

2. NRMA Profile

The National Retail Merchants Association (NRMA), based in New York City, is the largest trade association in the United States dedicated to research and education in general merchandise retailing—the most comprehensive organization for retail management.

A not-for-profit organization, NRMA serves retail firms of all sizes in the United States and around the world. Members include chains, department stores, mass merchandisers, specialty stores, and independent retailers.

When established in 1911, NRMA stated its mission as follows and it remains true today:
- to concentrate opinions upon matters affecting the economy and well-being of the industry
- to foster research, education, development and study
- to gather, collect and disseminate information and statistical data
- to distribute articles, treatises, periodicals and books particularly related to the distribution of goods at retail

Since 1911, retailers worldwide have been attracted to the benefits of NRMA membership. Today, U.S. store members number around 45,000 and distribute $150 billion in goods and services to consumers. The International Division serves over 5,000 stores in 50 countries abroad. Also included in the membership are associate members who provide services, equipment and merchandise to retailers.

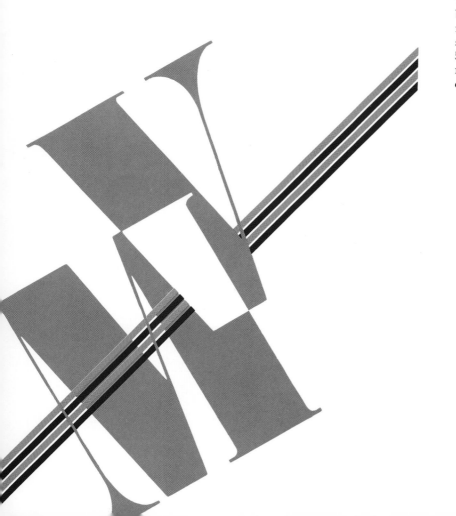

What NRMA Offers

1. EXPERTISE
   Professional counsel and assistance are available on all aspects of retail management from a vast merchandising complex to a single store.

2. IDEAS
   One-on-one consultation is available between NRMA's professional staff and store personnel. Meetings, seminars and conferences in every area from advertising to technology offer ideas on the latest trends.

3. EDUCATION
   Conferences, seminars, and workshops around the country discuss in detail all facets of retailing.

4. INFORMATION
   Members can receive valuable and authoritative publications concerning every aspect of specialty, independent, mass merchandising, and department store management and operation.

5. RESEARCH
   Major studies chart and appraise retailing's ever-changing course.

6. RESOURCES
   A constantly expanding library of NRMA literature is at member's disposal.

7. INSPIRATION
   An annual convention and trade exposition is held every January in New York City attracting delegates from around the globe. Major topics of worldwide importance are addressed by industry leaders and top economists.

8. TRENDS
   With membership—subscription to *STORES*—a stimulating, highly-acclaimed monthly magazine filled with authoritative articles on the latest retailing developments.

9. CLOUT
   The Washington staff conducts a continuous program to help make our government responsive to the needs of both retailers and consumers and aids members in interpreting the results.

10. GROUP BENEFITS
    Membership advantages include: group life, medical and workmen's compensation insurance plans; check guarantee program; group bank card program; leasing and location advisory service; transportation management program and auto rental discounts.

Professional Staff

NRMA committees and boards are supported by a professional staff which is organized along the lines of a well-run general merchandise store with an executive responsible for each of the major divisions: Credit Management, Information Systems, Financial Executives, Merchandising, Operations, Personnel and Sales Promotion-Marketing.

These divisional executives keep abreast of the latest developments in their particular fields of expertise. They initiate research studies, publish books and periodicals, and arrange for conferences, seminars and symposiums as well as providing individual consultation services to members.

How NRMA Functions

Direction and guidance come from the membership, through elected officers, directors, and an extensive committee system. Committees and board's of directors are composed of representatives from a cross section of the membership.

The NRMA Board of Directors is elected by the membership and is composed of over 100 retail executives representing stores of all sizes and types throughout the United States and other countries as well.

NRMA recognizes the importance of the independent stores which comprise the fastest growing segment of NRMA membership and so has created an Independent Stores Board of Directors made up of individual entrepreneurs.

For more information on the National Retail Merchants Association write to:

National Retail Merchants Association

100 West 31st Street,
New York, New York 10001
Phone: (212) 244-8780
Telex: INT'L 220-883-TAUR

Washington D.C. Office:
1000 Connecticut Avenue NW, 20036
Telephone: (202) 223-8250

3. NRMAS's Visual Merchandising Board Winners

1982
Andrew J. Markopoulos, svm

Dayton Hudson
Minneapolis, Minnesota

1983
Cecil Bessellieu, svm

Belk Stores Services
Charlotte, North Carolina

1984
Robert Benzio, svm

Saks Fifth Avenue
New York, New York

1985
Frank C. Calise, svm

Bonwit Teller
New York, New York

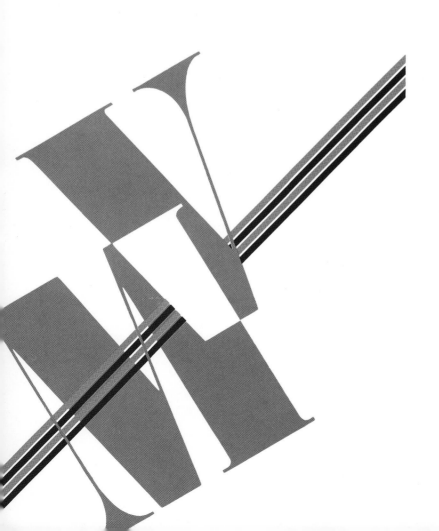

Frank C. Calise

Frank C. Calise

Robert Benzio

Andrew J. Markopoulos

project: G. B. Harb & Son, Los Angeles
design firm: L. A. Design
carpet: Royal Tartan by Bentley
photographer: Leland Lee

DuPont ANTRON® XL Nylon for low
maintenance and high performance

STEP INTO QUALITY

From the moment a customer walks in . . .
to the sale . . . there's a sense of quiet elegance
and high fashion with Bentley commercial carpets.

Step into quality when you choose Bentley
designer solids and patterns. Call your Bentley
Store Planning Specialist for a look
at high fashion, performance and style.

Quick delivery available for custom colors.

BENTLEY

BENTLEY MILLS, INC.   818-333-4585
14641 E. Don Julian Road   714-598-9768
City of Industry, CA 91746   800-423-4709

Display The Natural Way

Create original displays with Lundia's all natural MDL fixtures. The crisp Scandinavian design and the richness of solid wood give you the basis for a good-looking and practical fixture for all merchandise categories.

Whether it's toys or housewares, ceramics or wine, merchandise moves when you combine MDL shelving fixtures with your imagination. Over 60 standard combinations of height, depth and width will fit into your most creative arrangements. And those seasonal changes are simple with MDL. Easy set up and rearrangement is a Lundia trademark.

Make MDL a part of your merchandising plan. Ask for Lundia's free idea brochure today.

MDL
MERCHANDISE
DISPLAY LINE

One week's signs in less than a day!

Your new Sign Shop!

Store Signing enters the Electronic Age

Clean, fast, and incredibly cost-effective, the PACC® System II computerized signing system renders all other sign making methods obsolete.

Combining an IBM PC with a "high resolution" printer and Reynolds' exclusive field tested software, PACC eliminates messy inks, cleaners, and chemicals associated with traditional and phototypesetting methods.

PACC will dramatically reduce your labor costs. And PACC can transmit all your signs to branch stores via telephone or microwave, saving distribution costs.

The new PACC sign shop will enable you to gain a competitive edge by making your benefit copy signing:
- more effective and profitable
- more controllable and timely
- support your ad copy
- easier than ever before!

Printasign's Advanced Communication Concept

REYNOLDS PRINTASIGN CO. / 9830 San Fernando Road, Pacoima, California 91331 / (818) 899-5281

TORQUEFUSION™

THE SHOWOFF!

**Fashioned In Acrylic
Fastened With Steel**

We hate to showoff. But in order for you to appreciate the amazing benefits of our new TorqueFusion™ Acrylic Displays, we had to. Just a little.

We make your product look great. Our crystal clear acrylic enhances your products from every angle. And our hand crafted polished edges provide added customer protection. TorqueFusion™ eliminates tops, bottoms, backs, and load bearing glue seams used in standard display unit construction methods today.

We'll be around a long time. We guarantee it. Using threaded fasteners, TorqueFusion™ Displays provide both strength and durability unparalleled in the market today. However, if a replacement shelf is ever needed, simply unscrew the threaded fasteners and replace it. Sound simple. It is.

We're ready to go on arrival. TorqueFusion™ Displays are shipped completely assembled. Simply uncrate it and place your merchandise.

We have it now at DesignLab. TorqueFusion™ Displays. The Display Fixture line for the future, today. For further information contact Don Ballard at 800/222-6408.

DesignLab

DesignLab / 3023 Asbury Avenue / Charlotte, N.C. 28206 / Phone 704-376-2769

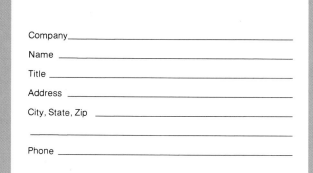

The Best of Store Designs

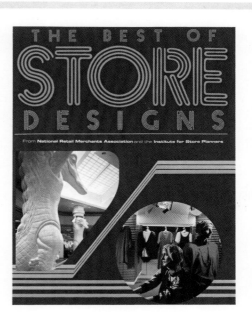

From the National Retail Merchants Association and
the Institute of Store Planners' Annual Design Competition

A new generation of affluent shoppers has sparked radical changes in the way retail stores are designed. The very best of these new designs are captured vividly in **The Best of Store Designs** in large, breathtaking photographs.

The winners of the annual NRMA/ISP retail store design competition are leaders of the new trends, using bold colors, and innovative treatments of fixtures and signage.

THE BEST OF
STORE DESIGNS
ISBN: 0-86636-012-3
Hardbound 9 x 12 in.
240 full-color pages
Over 100 photographs
and illustrations
$49.95
Available Now

The Best of Store Designs portrays the excitement generated by new designs and by renovations of department stores, hard goods retailers, specialty stores, and service establishments. Detailed text and captions give the background of each design and tells how it was executed. Credits list the store, the client, the designers, engineers, architects, fixtures suppliers, and interior designers.

Anyone who works with retail spaces will find **The Best of Store Designs** an essential guide to contemporary retail design.

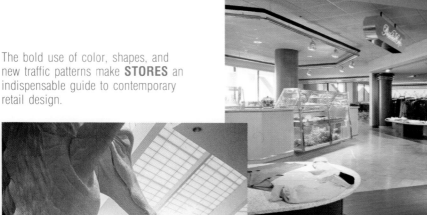

The bold use of color, shapes, and new traffic patterns make **STORES** an indispensable guide to contemporary retail design.

Actual floor plans show how the space was utilized for aisles, fixtures, storage, and selling area.

PBC INTERNATIONAL, INC. • One School Street, Glen Cove, New York 11542   Telephone: **(516) 676-2727** • Telex **499-6141**